F

Cookbook

Gretel Beer

ILLUSTRATED BY DES FOX

Appletree Press

First published in 1993 by
The Appletree Press Ltd,
19-21 Alfred Street,
Belfast BT2 8DL
Tel: +44 232 243 074 Fax: +44 232 246 756

A Little Hungarian Cookbook

For Peter Esterhazy

A catalogue record for this book is available
from the British Library.

ISBN 0-86281-362-X

9 8 7 6 5 4 3 2

Introduction

Hungarian cooking is rich and rare, spicy and beguiling. Stews warmed with paprika and mellowed with sour cream, cakes and pastries which rank among the most famous in the world — this little book can only present a small selection of the best, and best known, traditional dishes. Try them at home for a real taste of Hungary.

Since paprika runs like a warm, rich thread through so much Hungarian cooking, make sure that you use real Hungarian paprika on which the recipes are based. It comes in various strengths, ranging from very mild and sweet, usually labelled "exquisite delicate", to hot. Those most commonly found are marked "noble sweet" or "delicate sweet" or sometimes, in German, *"edelsüss"*, which are slightly hotter and recommended for most of the recipes given in this book. Quantities, as you will notice, are quite generous. "Rose" paprika, despite its name, is second from the top as far as fieriness is concerned. Never fry paprika — when it is added to onions browning in fat, for instance, always add liquid immediately to prevent the paprika turning black and bitter.

All flour used in the recipes is plain flour, unless otherwise stated. All butter is unsalted.

A note on measures
Metric and imperial measurements have been given for all the recipes. For perfect results use one set only. Spoon measurements are level except where otherwise indicated. Seasonings can of course be adjusted according to taste. Recipes are for four unless otherwise noted.

Korhelyleves

Thick Fish Soup

Hungarians use spicy Debrecen sausages for this deliciously thick soup; Spanish chorizo sausages make an adequate substitute.

1 lb/450g sauerkraut	3 strips bacon
1 lb/450g smoked pork	1 tbsp flour
(rib or loin)	1/2 lb/225g smoked
1 garlic clove, crushed	Hungarian sausage
1 medium-size onion, finely sliced	1 tbsp paprika
1 tbsp chopped dill	5 fl oz/140ml sour cream

(serves 6-8)

Drain sauerkraut, reserving the liquid, and cut through with a sharp knife to shorten the strands. Rinse smoked pork in cold water and pat dry with kitchen paper. Put the sauerkraut into a large pan, add smoked pork, onions, garlic and dill. Add plenty of water (about 4 pt/2 1/4 lt, bring to the boil and simmer until pork is tender. Take out the pork and cut into bite-size pieces.

Dice the bacon. Put the fat pieces into a frying pan first and fry lightly until the fat begins to run. Add the lean pieces and fry until golden brown and crisp. Lift out with a slotted spoon and drain on kitchen paper. Stir the flour into the bacon fat and brown; add a little lard or pork dripping if there is not enough rendered bacon fat. Stir in the paprika and immediately add 2–3 tablespoons water. Add this thickening to the sauerkraut together with its reserved juice, the bacon, chopped smoked pork and sliced sausages. Stir in the sour cream and simmer gently for 5 minutes. Adjust seasoning if necessary (the smoked pork may have contained enough salt).

Halászlé

Fish Soup

An authentic Hungarian fish soup which is practically a meal in itself.

1 carp, approx. 6 3/4 lb/3 kg or the equivalent in mixed freshwater fish	1 green pepper, de-seeded and sliced
1 lb/450g sliced onions	1/4 celeriac
1 garlic clove, crushed	2 tbsp paprika
	salt
	1 tsp tomato paste

(serves 6–8)

Clean, fillet and skin the fish, reserving skin and all trimmings and cut into chunks. Sprinkle fish chunks and roes (milt) with salt and set aside in a cool place. Put all fish trimmings, including the heads, into a large saucepan, add onions, garlic, green pepper, celeriac, parsley root, paprika and salt. Cover with 3 1/2 pt/2 lt water. Bring to the boil and simmer gently for 1 1/2 hours.

Put the fish chunks and roes (milt) into a large saucepan and strain the hot liquid over them; if necessary, skim off the fat first (carps heads in particular contain a lot of fat). Add the tomato purée and poach the fish gently in the liquid. Do not stir, but shake the pan very gently from time to time until the fish is just cooked. Adjust seasoning if necessary. Serve in warmed deep plates or bowls.

Cream or sour cream is not usually added, but this is optional. My Hungarian friends often crumble a small dried red pepper (a hot little cherry pepper, not a chilli) onto their plates before pouring the hot soup over it.

Bableves

Bean Soup

This is equally good made with broad beans or sliced French beans,
even when the latter are past their prime, in which case use only
the pods.

6oz/170g shelled broad beans or sliced French beans
2 1/4 pt/1 1/4 lt ham stock or water
1 heaped tbsp butter
5oz/140g diced smoked bacon
1 small finely chopped onion
1 scant tbsp flour
salt and pepper
4 tbsp sour cream

Simmer the beans in the lightly salted water or stock until tender.
Drain, reserving the liquid. Melt the butter in a pan and lightly
brown the bacon. Lift out with a slotted spoon. Add the chopped
onion to the pan and cook until softened. Dust with flour and
brown lightly. Add a little of the liquid from the beans, stir, and
add remaining liquid, beans and fried bacon. Bring to the boil and
simmer for 5 minutes. Season with salt and pepper. Swirl in the
sour cream just before serving.

Bográcsgulyás

Kettle Gulyas (Goulash)

Bográcsgulyás is one of the dishes that demands a paprika such as "rose" or "noble rose", just below the most fiery variety.

8oz/250g chopped onions	2 tbsp rose paprika
2 level tbsp lard	1 tomato, peeled, and
2 lb/900g stewing beef (shin,	quartered
chuck, leg of mutton cut),	2 green peppers, de-seeded
cubed	and sliced
1 clove garlic	8oz/250g potatoes, peeled
salt	and cubed
1 tsp caraway seeds	Galuska (see p. 12)

(serves 4–6)

Melt the lard in a thick saucepan and cook onions until soft. Add beef and stir over low heat for about 10 minutes, gently browning onions and meat. Crush garlic with a little salt, together with the caraway seeds. Add to the meat and onions. Remove from heat, stir in paprika and add tomato. Return saucepan to heat and add 4 pt/2¼ lt warm water, a little at a time. Cover with a lid, bring to the boil and simmer gently for 1–1½ hours, depending on the cut of meat and size of cubes.

Add green peppers, potatoes and a pinch of salt to the pan. Bring to the boil again and simmer for 25 minutes, until potatoes are tender.

Meanwhile prepare paste for *Galuska* (see p. 12). Cut out small balls of the paste with the help of a teaspoon and drop them into the boiling *Gulyás*. Simmer for a few minutes (the *Galuska* will rise to the top when cooked). Serve *Bográcsgulyás* in hot, deep plates.

Galuska (*Baby dumplings*) Very small dumplings which are cooked in soups or stews.

I egg
3 heaped tbsp flour
salt

Break the egg into a small bowl, add a pinch of salt and whisk lightly with a fork. Add flour to make a fairly smooth paste. Using a teaspoon, scoop out small quantities of the paste (about $1/4$ teaspoon) and drop into hot soup or stew, dipping the spoon into the hot liquid to release the little dumplings. They take only 2–3 minutes to cook, no more, and rise to the top when done.

Rácponty

Baked Carp

Whole carp or carp fillets can be used for this unusual dish.

I carp, approx. 3 lb/I $1/4$ kg	I tbsp paprika
$1/4$ lb/IIOg smoked bacon	2 tomatoes, peeled and sliced
I lb/450g potatoes	2 green peppers, de-seeded
salt	and sliced
I tbsp lard	2oz/50g melted butter
I medium-size onion,	5 fl oz/I40ml sour cream
thinly sliced	butter for the dish
(serves 4–6)	

Pre-heat oven to gas mark 5, 375°F, 190°C. Scale and clean the fish and lard with strips of smoked bacon; or cut into fillets, make a few incisions and push strips of bacon into the cavities. Parboil the

potatoes in their skins, peel and slice. Butter a large baking dish. Put the sliced potatoes into the dish, sprinkle with salt and arrange the whole carp, or carp fillets, on top. Salt very lightly.

Melt lard in a pan, add onion and cook until soft. Stir in paprika and immediately add 4 tablespoons water. Bring to the boil and stir. Add tomatoes, green peppers and a pinch of salt, and pour over the fish. Pour melted butter over the top and bake in the oven for 30 minutes. Pour in sour cream and bake for another 15–20 minutes at the same temperature. (Cooking times are for whole fish; if using fillets, reduce cooking times accordingly, depending on their size.)

Fogas bakonyi módra

Baked Pike/Perch with Wild Mushrooms

Fogas (pike/perch) could almost be called the "national" fish of Hungary. If you cannot get it, use any other firm-fleshed white fish.

I large pike or perch, approx. 3 1/2 lb/I 1/4 kg or the equivalent in smaller fish	*1/2 tbsp paprika*
	I tbsp flour
	9fl oz/250 ml sour cream
salt and peppercorns	*butter for the dish*
4oz/II0g butter	*I tbsp finely chopped green pepper or parsley*
4oz/II0g onions, finely sliced	
9oz/250g wild mushrooms, sliced	
(serves 4–6)	

Pre-heat oven to gas mark 5, 375°F, 190°C. Clean, fillet and skin the fish. Put skin, bones and head into a saucepan, cover with water and add salt and a few peppercorns. Bring to the boil and then simmer gently for $1/2$ hour. Rinse the fillets, pat dry with kitchen paper, and sprinkle with salt. Put the fillets into a buttered ovenproof dish.

Melt the butter in a pan, add onion and cook until soft, without browning. Add sliced mushrooms. Simmer over low flame until the mushrooms are cooked, add paprika and strain about a cupful of fish broth into the pan. Slake flour with sour cream, add to the pan and heat thoroughly. Season with salt and pour the mixture over fish fillets in the dish. Bake for about 30 minutes in the oven. Garnish with finely chopped green pepper or parsley before serving.

Borjupörkölt

Veal Pörkölt

Pörkölt is a rich stew which can be made with fish or meat.

---

2 tbsp lard	2 lb/1 kg veal (shoulder or leg)
2 medium-size onions,	cut into 1-inch cubes
finely sliced	salt
1 garlic clove, crushed	1 green pepper, de-seeded and
1 heaped tbsp paprika	sliced

(serves 4–6)

Melt the lard in a pan, add the onion and garlic and cook until onion is soft and transparent. Increase the heat to brown onion lightly, then stir in the paprika and immediately add 4 fl oz water. Stir to blend and cook gently for a minute or two, then add veal and salt. Cover and simmer over low heat, adding water in very small quantities and only if absolutely necessary to stop the meat from burning.

After 20 minutes add green pepper. Simmer until the meat is cooked, letting the liquid reduce towards the end of cooking time. There will not be much gravy but what there is should be superb.

Paprikás csirke

Paprika Chicken

Paprika chicken is one of the best known Hungarian dishes.

I chicken, 3–3 ¹/₂ lb/I¹/₂–I ³/₄ kg	salt
2oz/50g lard	2 tomatoes, peeled and
2 medium-size onions,	quartered
finely chopped	I level tbsp flour
2 green peppers, de-seeded and	4 fl oz/II0 ml sour cream
sliced separately	
I heaped tbsp paprika	

Wash, dry and joint the chicken into convenient pieces. Melt the lard in a pan, add the onions and cook until soft, without browning. Add one of the green peppers and cook very gently until soft, then stir in paprika and immediately add 4 fl oz of water. Stir, then add chicken pieces, turning them so that they are coated with onion and paprika. Add salt and tomato. Cover with a lid and simmer gently until the chicken is tender, adding water only if absolutely necessary.

Take out the chicken pieces and keep warm. Slake the flour with sour cream and about I tablespoon water, then add to the liquid in saucepan. Stir over low heat until well blended and thickened, then add remaining green pepper, and return chicken pieces to the pan. Simmer for another 5 minutes, adjusting seasoning if necessary. Transfer chicken pieces and sauce to a deep, warmed serving dish and spoon double cream over the top.

Szekelygulyás

Pork Stew with Sauerkraut

Quite often called *Szekelykáposzta* (*Szekely* cabbage) to emphasize the cabbage part of the dish.

---

2 lb/1 kg lean pork (shoulder)
2 tbsp lard
2 large onions, finely chopped
1 clove garlic, crushed
1 tsp caraway seeds
1 tbsp chopped fresh dill
stock or water
2 lb/1 kg sauerkraut
1 heaped tbsp paprika
salt
4 tbsp sour cream
(serves 6–8)

Dice the pork into 2oz/50 g pieces. Melt lard in a pan, add onions and garlic and cook until soft. Add pork, caraway seeds and dill. Stir over low heat, then cover the pan and simmer gently, adding just enough stock or water to cover, until the pork is half cooked.

Drain all moisture from the sauerkraut and add to the pork, together with the paprika. Simmer until meat and sauerkraut are cooked. Stir in salt to taste and spoon warmed sour cream over the top just before serving.

Majoránás tokány

Marjoram Tokány

Many different versions of *Tokány* can be found in Hungary, using beef, veal, pork or game; there is even one which includes goose liver.

---

2 lb/1 kg beef
3oz/85g lard
10oz/300g onions, finely sliced
1 tbsp fresh marjoram, finely chopped
salt and pepper
8 fl oz/¼ lt dry white wine
10oz/300g diced smoked bacon
8 fl oz/¼ lt sour cream
(serves 4–6)

Cut the beef into strips measuring about ¼ in x 1½ in (1 cm x 4 cm). Melt the lard in a pan, add onions and cook over low heat until soft. Turn up heat, add beef, and brown onions and beef together. Add marjoram, salt and pepper, stir, and add white wine. Leave to simmer until beef is half-cooked.

Meanwhile fry the bacon lightly in its own fat, then add to the beef and onion mixture, together with the sour cream. Simmer gently until the beef is cooked, reducing the liquid towards the end of cooking time if necessary.

Serpenyös rostélyos

Braised Steaks

Frying or braising steak will make this dish economical as well as delicious.

4 steaks, 7–8oz/200–225g each	I level tsp caraway seeds
salt	I–2 green peppers, de-seeded
2 tbsp lard	and sliced
8oz/250g onion, finely chopped	I large tomato, peeled and sliced
I clove garlic, crushed	I lb/450g potatoes, peeled and
I heaped tbsp paprika	diced

Pound the steaks to flatten them slightly, then make a few incisions round the edges to prevent curling. Dust lightly with salt.

Heat the lard in a frying pan large enough to hold the steaks side by side. Fry the steaks quickly on both sides, set aside and keep warm. Soften the chopped onion in the same fat, together with crushed garlic, then turn up the heat to brown the onion. Add paprika, caraway seeds and about half a cupful of water. Stir until well blended, then add the steaks, green peppers and tomato.

Cover the pan and simmer over low heat, adding water only if necessary, until steaks are almost cooked. Add diced potatoes with enough warm water to just cover them, and simmer gently until steaks and potatoes are tender.

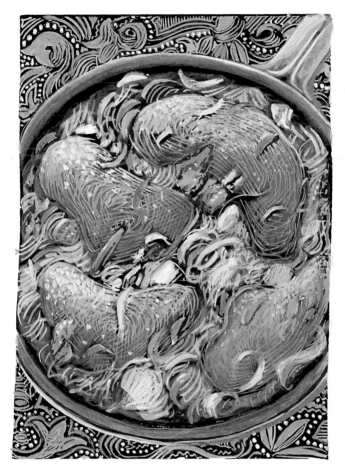

Lescó

Hungarian Ratatouille

Lescó can be served as a vegetable or a main dish when often sausages are added or some lightly beaten eggs scrambled into it just before serving.

---

2 tbsp lard
I large onion, sliced
I lb/450g green peppers, de-seeded and coarsely sliced
I lb/450g ripe tomatoes, skinned and quartered
$\frac{1}{2}$ tsp paprika
salt and sugar

Melt the lard in a pan, add sliced onion and allow to soften without browning. Add sliced green peppers and simmer gently for 10 minutes. Add tomatoes, paprika, salt and a pinch of sugar and simmer for 20–25 minutes. Serve immediately.

Variation: Chop 4oz/110g bacon and fry gently in the lard. Add sliced onion and cook in the rendered bacon fat until soft. Increase heat to brown onion and bacon together, then add sliced green peppers, tomatoes, salt, paprika and sugar. Simmer gently until the peppers are cooked.

Paradicsomos káposzta

Sweet and Sour Cabbage

An excellent way of cooking cabbage.

2oz/50g lard	dash of wine vinegar
1 small onion, sliced	salt and pepper
1 tbsp sugar	1 tsp caraway seeds
1 small white cabbage, approx.	6 tomatoes, peeled, and chopped
2 lb/1 kg, finely shredded	or 3 tbsp tomato paste
1/2 green pepper, de-seeded	4 fl oz/125 ml stock or water
and finely sliced	1 heaped tsp flour

Heat the lard in a pan, add onion and cook in the lard, without browning. When soft, sprinkle with sugar. Stir over medium heat until sugar turns golden brown, then throw in the cabbage and green peppers (stand away from the pan as contents are apt to splutter). Stir, then add a dash of wine vinegar, salt, pepper, caraway seeds, tomatoes or tomato purée and water or stock. Simmer gently until cabbage is cooked but still crisp. Adjust seasoning if necessary — there should be a definite sweet/sour flavour. Slake flour with a little water, add to cabbage and simmer for another 5 minutes.

Tejfeles tökkáposzta

Vegetable Marrow With Dill and Sour Cream

Vegetable marrow tastes quite different when cooked the Hungarian way.

---

1 vegetable marrow, approx. 3 lb/1.5 kg
salt
2 tbsp butter
1/2 small onion, finely chopped
2 scant tbsp flour
2 tbsp fresh dill, finely chopped
8 fl oz/225 ml stock or water
scant 1/4 pt/125 ml sour cream
wine vinegar, pinch of sugar
(serves 4–6)

Peel and quarter the marrow, remove seeds. Shred or grate the marrow flesh, sprinkle with salt and leave to stand for 1/2 – 3/4 hour. Meanwhile melt the butter, add the chopped onion and cook in the butter until soft, then brown very lightly. Dust with flour, stir, then add chopped dill. Stir in stock or water to make a thick sauce. Simmer for a few minutes until well blended.

Squeeze out all the moisture from the marrow and add the flesh to the sauce. Stir in sour cream, and simmer for 20–30 minutes. Add vinegar and sugar, taste and add salt if necessary.

Tarhonya

Hungarian Pasta

9oz/250g flour
good pinch of salt
2–3 eggs

Sift flour and salt into a bowl. Whisk the eggs lightly and work into the flour gradually, until you have small uneven pieces of dough. Leave to dry a little, then rub through a fairly large-holed metal sieve. Use up all the dough in this way, working together any left-over pieces with a little water and pushing them through the sieve as before. Spread out the little grain-size pellets over a table covered with a tablecloth and leave to dry for several days until practically rock hard. Move pasta gently from time to time so that it is all exposed to the air. Store in a screw-top jar, where it will keep for a long time. *Tarhonya* is used in soups, sprinkled directly into the hot liquid, or as an accompaniment to meat, when it is usually prepared like this:

---

3 ¹/₂ oz/100g lard	*salt*
I small onion, finely chopped	*I tsp paprika*
9oz/250g Tarhonya	*3¹/₂ oz/100g diced smoked bacon*

If baking, pre-heat the oven to gas mark 5, 375°F, 190°C. Melt the lard in a flameproof casserole and gently cook the finely sliced onion in the fat until soft. Add *Tarhonya* and brown lightly together with the onion. Add salt and paprika and cover with stock or water. Cover with a lid and leave to simmer gently for about 15 minutes or until all the liquid has been absorbed, or bake in the oven. Serve sprinkled with crisply fried, diced bacon.

Tepertös pogácsa

Crackling Biscuits

Thick savoury biscuits which make a splendid snack, accompanied by a glass of beer or wine. If you don't have time to render pork fat at home, use pork crackling from a roast.

11oz/300g pork crackling	3oz/100g lard
1oz/30g fresh yeast	2 eggs
3 tbsp tepid milk	2 tbsp sour cream
18oz/500g strong flour	dash of brandy or rum
1/2 tbsp salt	1 egg yolk to glaze
(makes 15)	

Chop the pork crackling finely by hand. Cream the yeast and mix with tepid milk and 1 teaspoon of the flour. Set aside to prove in a warm place.

Sift remaining flour with a pinch of salt and work to a soft dough with the chopped lard, eggs, sour cream and a dash of brandy or rum. Work in the chopped pork crackling. Set the dough in a warm place until doubled in bulk.

Roll out dough on a floured board, fold into three and allow to rest for 10 minutes. Repeat rolling, folding and resting twice more, then roll out to the thickness of a finger. Cut into rounds, of about 2 in/5 cm diameter. Set aside to rise for about half an hour. Pre-heat oven to gas mark 5, 375°F, 190°C.

Mark the top of the biscuits in a criss-cross pattern with the back of a knife and brush with egg yolk mixed with a little water. Let the glaze dry a little, then bake in the oven on a buttered, floured baking sheet until golden brown.

Töltött paprika

Stuffed Green Peppers

Tomato sauce:	
1 small onion	2 lb/1 kg ripe tomatoes
2 tbsp oil or 1 tbsp lard	salt, pepper, sugar, lemon juice
2 scant tbsp flour	5 fl oz/140ml tomato juice
Stuffed peppers:	
4 large or 8 small green peppers	salt, pepper, 1 tbsp chopped
1 tbsp lard	parsley
1 small onion	3/4 lb/350g minced lean beef
2oz/50g rice	and pork, mixed
	1 egg

To make the tomato sauce: chop the onion, heat oil or butter in a heavy saucepan, and cook the onion until soft without browning. Dust the onion with flour and brown very lightly. Add broken up tomatoes, salt, pepper, a good pinch of sugar (this depends on the ripeness of the tomatoes), lemon juice, and tomato juice. Stir well and simmer until the tomatoes are pulpy — about 30 minutes.

Meanwhile, cut off and reserve the tops of the green peppers, and remove the seeds and white fibres. In a bowl, pour boiling, slightly salted water over green peppers and their tops, leave for 5 minutes, and drain them. Melt the butter, add finely chopped onion. Cook until soft. Add the rice. Stir over low heat until rice is transparent. Add 3/4 cup water, cover the pan, and simmer until the water has been absorbed (the rice should be half-cooked). Leave to cool a little, then mix with the meat, salt, pepper, chopped parsley and egg. Three-quarter fill the green peppers with the meat mixture (the filling will swell during the cooking) and replace pepper tops. Stand the filled peppers in a deep

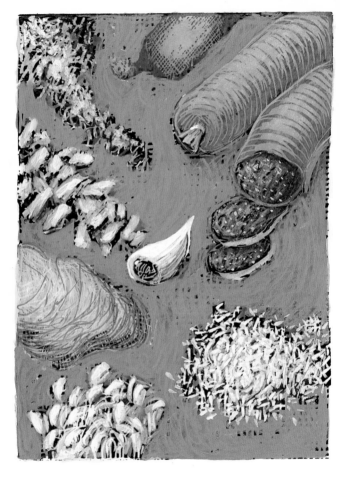

casserole dish. If there is any filling left over, form into small balls and place around the peppers. Sieve the tomato sauce and pour over the peppers together with all the liquid — the sauce should be fairly thin. Cover casserole dish with a lid and cook over very low heat or at gas mark 3, 325°F, 160°C for about 1 hour. Taste sauce before serving and adjust seasoning if necessary, adding a little more sugar and/or lemon juice.

Rakott káposzta

Layered Sauerkraut and Pork Casserole

1 ½ lb/675g sauerkraut	1 tbsp paprika
8 fl oz/225 ml ham stock	salt
2 tbsp lard, plus small quantity	5oz/140g diced smoked bacon
for greasing casserole	5oz/140g sliced smoked
1 medium-size onion, chopped	Hungarian sausage
1 clove garlic, crushed	3oz/85g parboiled rice
1 lb/450g lean minced pork	8 fl oz/225 ml sour cream

(serves 6)

Pre-heat oven to gas mark 5, 375°F, 190°C. Rinse the sauerkraut under cold water, unless it is very mild. Cook sauerkraut in ham stock for about 15 minutes. Grease a deep ovenproof casserole with butter. Melt 1 ½ tablespoons of the lard, soften onion and garlic in this, then add the meat, paprika and salt and brown everything together, breaking up the meat with a fork as it browns. Melt remaining butter, add diced bacon, and heat until the fat runs, then fry lightly, together with the sliced sausage. Put a third of the sauerkraut into the casserole, top with half the sausage and bacon, a thin layer of parboiled rice, and half the meat. Add half the sour cream, cover with another third of the sauerkraut and proceed as before, finishing with a layer of sauerkraut. Pour remaining sour cream over the top. Bake for 45–50 minutes.

Csúsztatott palacsinta

"Slipped" Pancakes

Light, downy pancakes piled high, with almond filling, topped with sour cream and baked like a cake.

Pancakes:
5 eggs	2oz/60g self-raising flour
2oz/60g icing or caster sugar	2oz/60g melted butter
6 fl oz/170 ml milk	

Filling:
3 eggs	butter and fine breadcrumbs
3 tbsp icing sugar	for the cake tin
a little grated lemon rind	6 fl oz/170 ml sour cream for
½ tsp vanilla sugar	topping
4oz/115g ground almonds	icing sugar
butter for frying	

(serves 4–6)

Butter a 9-inch spring-clip cake tin and dust lightly with fine breadcrumbs. Pre-heat oven to gas mark 6, 400°F, 200°C.

To make the batter, separate egg yolks and whites. Whisk egg yolks with sugar until thick and creamy. Whisk in the milk. Whisk egg whites until stiff and fold into the batter alternately with the sifted flour. Fold in the melted, but not hot, butter.

To make the filling, separate egg yolks and whites. Whisk egg

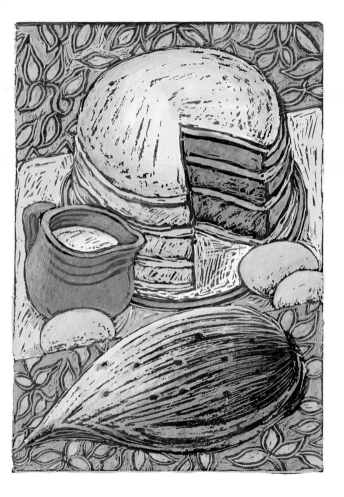

yolks with sugar until thick and creamy; add grated lemon rind and vanilla sugar. Whisk egg whites until stiff and fold into the egg yolks alternately with the ground almonds.

Melt a small knob of butter in a frying pan (if possible the same size or slightly smaller than the cake tin). Pour in a quarter of the batter and fry the pancake until golden brown on one side. Do not fry it on the other side. Slip the pancake upside down into the cake tin so the uncooked side rests on the bottom. The first pancake is quite easy as you can simply invert the cake tin over the frying pan. The others are a little more difficult. If necessary, push the pancakes gently into place. Spread the cooked side of each pancake with filling before placing the next pancake on top, finishing with a pancake. Spread sour cream thickly over the top and bake the pudding for about 20–25 minutes until the cream is just tinged with colour. Remove from the oven, release the spring-clip and dust the top of the gâteau thickly with icing sugar. Do not attempt to remove it from the base. Set it on a serving dish. Serve warm, cut into wedges.

Túrós gombóc

Sweet Cottage Cheese Dumplings

Sweet dumplings and pasta dishes make favourite Hungarian puddings.

3 eggs	1 tbsp flour
2 tbsp butter	3 tbsp butter
salt	3oz/100g fine breadcrumbs

18oz/500g cottage cheese, drained and sieved	4 fl oz/100 ml sour cream icing sugar mixed with a little
2oz/50g semolina	vanilla sugar
1 tbsp cream or sour cream	

(serves 4–6)

Separate egg yolks and whites. Cream butter with a pinch of salt until light and fluffy, beat in the egg yolks one by one, then add sieved cottage cheese, semolina and cream or sour cream. Leave to stand for half an hour.

Bring a large pan of lightly salted water to the boil. Whisk egg whites until stiff and fold into the dough alternately with the flour. Shape a test dumpling about the size of a table tennis ball and drop into the boiling water. Simmer for 6 minutes, drain and cut open to see if it is cooked through. Adjust cooking time accordingly. Form remaining dough into dumplings and cook as before, then drain carefully.

Melt butter and fry breadcrumbs until golden brown then sprinkle over the dumplings or roll them in the browned breadcrumbs. Place on a warm plate, pour sour cream over the top and dust with vanilla-scented icing sugar.

Réstestészta

Strudel Pastry

Almost every Hungarian housewife has her own special formula for making perfect strudel pastry. This version includes sour cream as the "magic" ingredient that makes it particularly easy to pull out the dough to paper thinness.

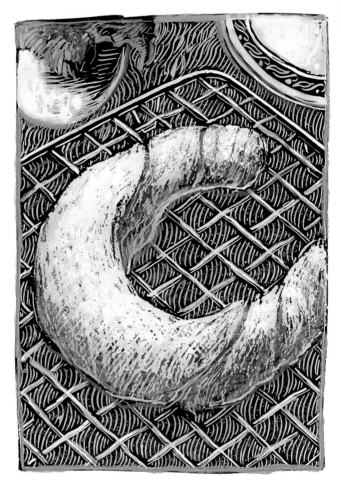

9oz/250g flour
good pinch of salt
1 egg yolk
3 1/2 fl oz/100 ml lukewarm water
3 1/2 fl oz/100 ml sour cream
1 tbsp salad oil
melted butter

Everything connected with the making of strudel pastry should be warm: working surfaces, hands, water. If you have to use a laminated, enamelled or marble pastry board wipe over it with a cloth wrung out in hot water before starting (a wooden-topped kitchen table is best).

Sift flour and salt onto a pastry board, make a well in the centre and drop in egg yolk and oil. Add warm water and sour cream, and knead to a soft dough. Work the dough well, bringing it down onto the pastry board with a few sharp slaps from time to time, until the dough is soft and pliable. Pat dough into a round, brush lightly with melted butter and cover with a warmed bowl (do not let the bowl touch the dough). Stand in a warm place, renewing the covering bowl if it cools too rapidly. Meanwhile prepare the required filling.

After half an hour the dough should be ready to be pulled out. Cover a large kitchen table, or dining table, with a clean cloth and sprinkle it with flour. Place the dough on the cloth and carefully roll it out as far as it will go, then slip your hands underneath the dough and pull it (use the backs of your hands and balls of thumbs, never the fingers) always working from the centre, and taking care not to tear the dough. When it is pulled out to paper thinness, brush it very lightly with melted butter and leave to dry for 10–15 minutes before using.

Almás rétes

Apple Strudel

Hungarian strudels range from sweet to savoury but Apple Strudel remains one of the most popular.

strudel pastry (see p. 44)	3oz/85g fine fresh breadcrumbs
2 lb/1 kg cooking apples, peeled, cored, and thinly sliced	2 tbsp butter
1 tbsp lemon juice	1–2 tbsp apricot jam
4oz/100g caster or icing sugar	4oz/100g melted butter
1 tbsp vanilla sugar	butter and flour for the baking sheet
4oz/100g raisins or sultanas	icing sugar
good pinch each ground cinnamon, nutmeg, and cloves	

Prepare strudel pastry as described on page 44. Pre-heat oven to gas mark 4, 350°F, 180°C. Place sliced apples in a bowl, sprinkle with lemon juice and add sugar, vanilla sugar, raisins and spices. Mix well, cover and set aside. Fry breadcrumbs in butter until golden brown. Sprinkle fried breadcrumbs evenly over the rolled-out pastry dough, then spread the apple and raisin filling over one third of the surface and dot with a little apricot jam. Sprinkle half the melted butter over the whole surface. Tear off the thick rim of pastry which should overhang the table and start rolling up the strudel by lifting the cloth at the end spread with filling. Roll up the pastry very carefully, like a Swiss roll, and secure the ends. Transfer strudel to a buttered and floured baking sheet, bending the strudel lightly to form a horseshoe. Brush with remaining melted butter and bake in the oven for 40–50 minutes. If the top browns too quickly, cover it very lightly with buttered greaseproof paper for part of the baking time, but remove the paper towards the end. Sprinkle with icing sugar while still warm.

Rigó jancsi

Chocolate Cream Slices

Delicious chocolate pastry, with chocolate filling as well as topping.

Pastry:	
generous 2 oz/60g plain chocolate	3 1/2 oz/100g granulated sugar
1 1/2 oz/40g butter	4 1/2 oz/120g flour
4 eggs	2 tbsp apricot jam
Filling:	
9 fl oz/250 ml double cream	4 1/2 oz/120g flour
Topping:	
6 fl oz/160 ml water	1 scant oz/20g butter
6oz/160g granulated sugar	4 1/2 oz/120g plain chocolate

Pre-heat oven to gas mark 6, 400°F, 200°C.

For the pastry, break the chocolate into small pieces, place in a small bowl with the butter and set over steam to soften. Remove from heat and leave to cool. Whisk eggs and sugar over steam until thick and fluffy, remove from heat and whisk until cool. Lightly fold in the flour and finally the softened butter and chocolate. Spread about 1/2 in/1 cm thick on baking sheets lined with buttered and floured baking paper. Bake in the oven for 10–12 minutes. Remove paper. Cut pastry into slices and then cut half the slices into squares.

To make the filling, put cream and grated chocolate into a small thick saucepan and bring to the boil slowly, stirring constantly. Leave to rise once, remove from heat and stir until cool. Chill well, then whisk lightly until it will just hold its shape (if whisked too much it will turn into chocolate butter).

To make the icing, put water and sugar into a small saucepan, stir over low heat until sugar dissolves, then bring to the boil and cook to small thread stage. Break chocolate into small lumps and set over steam to soften. Beat in butter, slowly stir in hot sugar solution and stir until smooth and shiny.

Spread the pastry squares with warmed apricot jam and then glaze with chocolate icing. Spread pastry slices thickly with cream filling, at least twice the thickness of the pastry. Place glazed squares on top and cut through so that you have cream-filled squares.

Csokoládétorta

Chocolate Gâteau

The original recipe, written on paper yellowed with age, is headed "Very good, recipe from Kugler-Gerbeaud" — one of the best pâtisseries in the world.

Cake:

6 eggs	5oz/140g icing sugar
3 ½ oz/85g plain chocolate	butter and flour for the cake tin
3 tbsp water	5oz ground, unblanched almonds
generous 2oz/60g butter	

Filling:

generous 2oz/60g unblanched almonds	I tbsp icing sugar
5oz/140g plain chocolate	5oz/140g butter
4 tbsp water	I heaped tbsp vanilla sugar
	2 egg yolks

Pre-heat oven to gas mark 4 1/2, 360°F, 185°C. Butter and flour a 10-inch spring-clip cake tin. To make the cake, separate yolks and whites of five of the eggs. Break the chocolate into small pieces and put into a small, heavy saucepan with the water. Stir over low heat until the chocolate melts. Remove pan from heat and leave to cool. Cream together butter and sugar until very light and fluffy, then beat in the five egg yolks, one by one. Cream well after each addition. Beat in the cooled chocolate and the sixth egg. Whisk egg whites until stiff, fold into the mixture, alternately with the ground almonds. Spoon mixture into the prepared cake tin and bake for 50—60 minutes. Test the cake before taking it out of the oven and leave it to cool a little in the tin before turning out, upside down, onto a wire rack to cool completely.

To make the filling, put the almonds on a baking sheet and brown them lightly in the oven. The oven temperature does not matter greatly, as long as you watch the almonds and do not allow them to scorch. Grind the almonds. Break the chocolate into small pieces, put into a heavy saucepan, add water and sugar, and stir over low heat until chocolate and sugar have dissolved completely. Cook very gently until the mixture has thickened slightly, remove from heat, and leave to cool. Cream butter with vanilla sugar until light and fluffy, then beat in the cooled chocolate and the egg yolks. Finally, stir in the ground browned almonds, reserving some to decorate the top and sides of the cake, if desired.

Cut through the cake once and spread it with half the chocolate filling. Spread remaining chocolate cream over top and sides.

Dobos torta

Dobos Gâteau

Created by Joszef C. Dobos in 1887, this has become one of the most famous confections in the world, a truly luscious gâteau where the thickness of the cream filling should about equal that of the pastry.

Pastry:
4 ¹/₂ oz/120g flour
6 eggs
5oz/140g icing sugar
1 tsp vanilla sugar
Filling:
3oz/85g plain chocolate
6oz/170g butter
4 ¹/₂ oz/120g icing sugar
2 tbsp vanilla sugar
1 egg
Caramel top:
5 ¹/₂ oz/150g granulated sugar
about 2 tbsp water
small knob of butter

Pre-heat oven to gas mark 7, 425°F, 220°C. To make the pastry, sift the flour twice. Separate egg yolks and whites. Whisk egg yolks with half the icing sugar until thick and creamy. Whisk egg

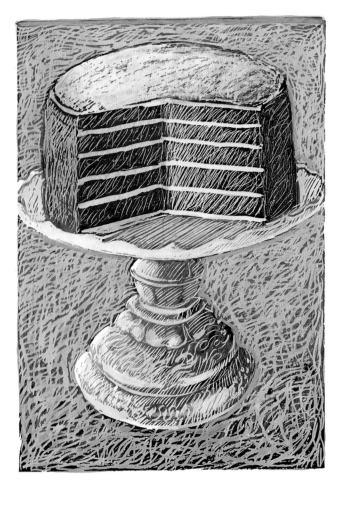

whites until stiff, fold in all remaining sugar, and whisk until smooth and shiny. Fold egg whites into egg yolks, alternately with the flour. Trace out 9 in/23 cm circles on 5 or 6 sheets of greaseproof paper. Butter the pieces of paper, dust with flour, and set on larger-size baking trays. Spread the mixture onto the pieces of paper and bake until golden brown (about 10 minutes). If possible, bake all layers at the same time. Remove carefully from paper and set to cool. When quite cold, place pastry circles between sheets of waxed or greaseproof paper, cover with a board, and weigh down.

For the filling, break the chocolate into small pieces and set to melt in a warm place. Cream butter with sugar and vanilla sugar until light and fluffy. Beat in the softened, but not hot, chocolate and finally beat in the egg.

Set aside the best-looking pastry circle. Sandwich together remaining circles with the filling, spreading it over the top and sides of the pastry as well. Take the reserved circle and set it on a work top brushed lightly with melted butter or dusted with flour.

For the topping, put the sugar and water in a small pan and set over low heat to dissolve. Stir in a small knob of butter. When the sugar has dissolved, increase heat and cook until golden brown. Remove from heat, and spoon quickly over the reserved pastry circle. Mark into portions at once, using a knife frequently dipped into hot water and run quickly over butter. If the sugar top has hardened too quickly, place the pastry circle in a warm oven for a few seconds to soften the sugar again, then mark as described. Place the caramelized circle on top of the gâteau.

Index

Almás rétes 48
Apple strudel 48

Bableves 8
Baked pike/perch with wild
    mushrooms 15
Baked carp 12
Bean soup 8
Bográcsgulyás 11
Borjupörkölt 16
Braised steaks 24

Crackling biscuits 35
Chocolate cream slices 51
Chocolate gâteau 52
Csokoládétorta 52
Csúsztatott palacsinta 40

Dobos gâteau 56
Dobos torta 56

Fish soup 7
Fogas bakonyi módra 15

Galuska (Baby dumplings) 12

Halászlé 7
Hungarian pasta 32
Hungarian ratatouille 27

Kettle gulyas (Goulash) 11
Korhelyleves 4

Layered sauerkraut and pork
    casserole 39
Lescó 27

Marjoram tokány 23
Majoránás tokány 23

Paprika chicken 19
Paprikás csirke 19
Paradicsomos káposzta 28
Pork stew with sauerkraut 20

Rácponty 12
Rakott káposzta 39
Réstestészta 44
Rigó jancsi 51

Serpenyös rostélyos 24
"Slipped" pancakes 40
Strudel pastry 44
Stuffed green peppers 36
Sweet and sour cabbage 28
Sweet cottage cheese
    dumplings 43
Szekelygulyás 20

Tarhonya 32
Tejfeles tökkáposzta 31
Tepertös pogácsa 35
Thick fish soup 4
Töltött paprika 36
Túrós gombóc 43

Veal pörkölt 16
Vegetable marrow with dill and
    sour cream 31